HORSES AND ORANGES

HORSES AND ORANGES

poems by Kirsten Garbini

Publication © Hands-On Books 2024
Text © Kirsten Garbini 2024
First published in 2024 by Hands-On Books
www.modjajibooks.co.za

ISBN 978-1-991240-42-2

Cover artwork: Jess Zlotnick
Front cover design: Monique Oberholzer
Book design and layout: Liz Gowans

Set in AA Smart Sans

CONTENTS

Author's note   7

1. Knitting with words

Pastry Maker	10
My best ballerina poem	11
Shopping list	12
Poem recipe	13
Don't be good.	14
Skin	15
Treasure	16
Poems in my dreams	17
Write	18
Speak my language	19
The why of us	20
Words	21

2. Thank you for Horses

Horses and oranges	24
Khaki fever	25
A girl's protest	26
Safe	27

3. Motherhood: The guts and the glory

Single mother with elephant	30
My boys	32
Mother's Day	33
Now that you are 21	35
The Love of You	36

4. In the branches

The softness of death	38
The cupboard	39
Initiation	40
My recipe book	42
Crow	43

5. Corporate moments

CEO moment	46
Two real-life movies	47
Job description: Lion tamer	49
C-Suite	51
In spite of the NDA.	52
Women in suits	53

7. Another Life

The dream suburb	56
I pronounce my body alive.	57
Carlotti	58
ICU	59
Tanya	60
Nancy Reagan	61
When healing comes	62
The trees and me	63
Asymmetry	64
The dream	65
My man Loneliness	67

8. I'm ready to travel

To us	70
Instant life	71
Wollumbin Retreat	72
Last day	73
Last poem	74

Afterword   75

Author's note

I begin, as my friends do, by recognising the profound significance of my homeland, South Africa, and the district of Ugu, where I now live. I express my gratitude for the wisdom and inspiration, with which this country and nation have influenced these poems.

As a South African woman of European descent, I am aware of my position as an intergenerational visitor here. With a heart open to learning and a spirit committed to understanding, I stand in solidarity with those who hold this broken, yearning-to-be-healed land dear, and I have done my best to engage with its heritage sensitively, humbly and reverently. This was the place where most of these poems gathered.

My palms are scratched deep with lines from my own ancestors' writing. We write. In the scattered bloodline, we write. When I write, my body becomes soil and I know my birthright is shared with all births on this earth.

When I write I am given clues to an ancient cell life presenting itself, while we assemble ourselves into clothes, drink coffee and become entranced by what we see in the mirror. The mirror, reflecting the who am I today, who forever, who never. Seeing the knowledge, corruption, and the treacherous beauty of our expanding identities. Where and when do we focus our kaleidoscope eyes? All these opportunities terrify and excite me. I want to catch them in my poems – writing is the only net I have.

1.
Knitting with words

Pastry Maker

God was a pastry maker
having a bad dream.
In his nightmare anguish
he kneaded and pounded,
aerating the dough.
He threw it up and down
and woke up, sweating,
dishevelled, upset.
In the morning,
there stood a naked man.
It was Adam.
The flour still on his shoulders.

My first poem, which I wrote when I was 12.

My best ballerina poem

The best poem I could write
would look like a ballerina tapping
pointe silk on hard, wooden floors.
The toe sound, the jump sound,
creating arcs with long, pink, stockinged legs.
No music, so you could hear the swish of silk,
the elegance of the invitation.
You - sitting lumpy, bulgy or veined,
would find your body asking
for a stretch, a fine leg line
Your own body now seeking
to be bold word strokes
in the silence.

Shopping list

A poem is the opposite
of a shopping list,
although both may present
succulent strawberries,
and people quietly going about
their own business in the world.

I want my shopping
lists to remind me that poetry insists
words become food,
lists become meals,
poems become
buffets of history.

Poem recipe

This is an invitation to you
to read the poem
that is written on your own heart.
I extend this call to read the words
in your heart cave,
in a language you know -
it's just the font you forgot.
The first breath you took
clouded the script,
but the sacred letters dream there,
of your awakening.
You see a few lines
like a wing, like a hoof print,
like the scent of a night garden.
To proceed:
bless the revelation before
you receive it
Stand on the brink of gratitude.
Mix
12 mm the infinite
30g your being
add 72 names of God.
Tear this page.
I can't help you at all.
I only do hypnosis with horses.

Don't be good.

Poems don't have to be good.
They just have to be themselves.
They're a moment of
throwing open the covers,
saying "jump in".
With long limbs next to yours.
And then the wonder
of who's going
to touch first.

Skin

I talk about birds,
the messages they bring,
like newspaper headlines.

I remark on the texture
of the blue cup on the table,
in a frozen tai chi stance
between the sugar and the milk.
I want the poetry of unspoken silence,
and to ask where dreams come from.

He drinks tea, crunches almonds, whispers
about how quickly we could undress,
and the urgency
of his desire and asks,
if I would only focus
on what mattered to him,
instead of on poems,
wanting
skin.

Treasure

What is the push,
asking hip bones to open, to bear down
on these words, overstaying their welcome
in my flesh?
In the writing, the relief
of sinew and breath made ink,
creation sistered, edges coloured,
now a simple,
hand-painted arc, flying
free on a canvas.
Free to be read,
broken like bread, eaten.
In the warm afternoon,
words bask, drink
talk in their own way,
join hands to hold
you, yes you, this day.
Bring water, bring words,
the yeast of your life –
let's make a poem.

Poems in my dreams

I was a murderer at 6,
a thief at 7,
at 8 I had lovers,
by 9 I was a gunslinger.
I took scalps.
I knew cowboys
didn't cry,
and I knew why.

It took me 56 years to discover
I was not immortal,
and that all my poems
were sleeping in my dreams,
and I could wake them
with innocent kisses.

Write

I claim a page
in my workbook
for a poem.
It is an act of disobedience.

The fresh poem
blinks at me.
A creative dislocation
in a book of tasks.

That night I dream of all my poems,
written on scraps of paper,
stuffed in a leopard-print bag.

We want out, they say softly. It's time.
Each scrap now with wing-folds
flies up like a flock of origami.
My poems delight in this rebel act.
They all escape.
Later I see a note on the fridge.
It's from the poems.
I stare at the font, the size,
the upright letters.
The anarchy of it:

"Get over your alphabet of
obstacles," it says.
"Write".

Speak my language

Do you speak my language?
Do poems sprout
between your footsteps
like sweet peas looking for a trellis?
Do stones shout,
"Take me home and love me?"
Do mountains mock and tease you
for being lonely, while they
unveil their nakedness
in the sunshine?
Do words make skin
upon your bones, dressing you in
the glory
of "let there be".

My pen is touched by
soldier, seer, beggarman, thief,
and I lift up my arms,
not knowing how else to revere
the beauty of the syllables.

Like fireflies, they cluster
at the bottom of the garden, near the ferns,
they swirl skywards, like a lighthouse
showing me the way.
I'm coming across the dark water
only to hear your poems,
your silence and the beauty of
your tongue.

The why of us

One reason why
it is essential to forever
seek the Holy Grail
– even if it's a smashed up,
dirty old cup – is to keep our demons at bay.

My sister holds incense and beads
She knows the Sanskrit of being, she
speaks with glitter breath and
has named each of her guitars
after a singing sage.

I am the sister that just makes poems,
like a blacksmith cook
exploring the messy kitchen, who has
the spaghetti-stained-white-shirt-job
of being an intern to words

We know the holy grail is broke.
It's now a Rubik's cube.
Whatever you seek requires three twists,
four turns, two sisters and a guitar called Narada Muni.

Words

My father, once an English teacher,
unpacked the box,
eventually putting the needle
on the vinyl.
I waited,
like it was Christmas morning.
A man's voice began,
in even, slow loops,
speaking warm, measured words,
words that rose up, up,
above the ceiling of the small house,
each of them glowing
with could-be-ness and
is-ness all at once.
I followed their balloon path,
watching the delicate
light of the sounds rising,
until I heard the very last two words –
a name:
Dylan Thomas.
It's a poem,
my dad said, smiling.
Let's hear it again, said I,
he's letting all the words free!
And just like that, words began to jostle me,
like prisoners, begging,
every other day, for a page, for a nod,
to be free.

2.

Thank you for Horses

Horses and oranges

When I'm on a horse,
I remember who I am,
feeling each of her four legs
touching the sand
in rhythmic tune.

She breathes, moves, waits
for my body to command her.
I speak a clear, wordless language,
that in each second connects us

– opens the moment up,
slicing it like an orange,
revealing pips,
so that the thick rind skin of that
instant is peeled back
and the next, next, next –

until a taste of eternity
fills my mouth,
and the crisp beauty
of being alive
runs its juice
down my throat.

Khaki fever

We met at a party.
You spoke about tracking
leopards at night,
and how women fall
in love with game rangers,
calling it "khaki fever".
I spoke about the rain
and horses.
Later, you sent me a photo,
a map of your body.
It was not somewhere
I was travelling to.
I had no plans
to get lost there,
as you suggested.
I didn't want the
free travel tips,
or advice for
first time visitors.
Instead, I got
instant jet lag
and a tummy bug
at the thought.
My diagnosis –
a common, suburban
variety of highly contagious,
khaki-induced,
toilet-cubicle fever.

A girl's protest

The rock was my home.
The tree my horse.
A place of stone-quiet aloneness.

I climbed the black branches
and would ride crazy on fire, into a story
that started with my mother's,
because I couldn't find my own.

My face is plain, she said.
Although I won the French prize,
and was head girl.
Hers was face of hand-me-downs
and never-minds.

I urged my horse branch
into clouds, sky, spirit,
into sunshine where nobody cared
about pretty or plain,
where everyone was blessed.
 I knew at ten years old
that being a girl was hard,
and being a woman meant
being on guard.

I developed a taste for the untamed.
I chose words seeking a mouth
I looked for fire stories in the sky.

I was almost 19 when I was asked to
try and be prettier
for men.
I opted for the badlands of
come say that here, instead.

Safe

The chafing on fresh red calves,
burned by horse riding,
the discomfort of falling,
bumping atop a horse called
Pebbles or Patti, hooves too loud,
saddle too pointy,

snorting, veering, branches
intent on swift beheadings,
welcoming your mad speed in thickets –

that is my safe space, simply because
it was a place you
were scared of, Dad.

3.

Motherhood: The guts and the glory

Single mother with elephant

That poet's-sky day lives in my heart:
a blue that asks for praise.
Three in Kruger,
my two sons, and I.

A long yellow grass day,
hot birds, lazy impala, and sugar air.
Elephants, none to be seen.
I stop next to a scraggy tree
just long enough
to make up the Lelefante song,
on the spot.

I call deep
from our ancientness to theirs,
from our shared birthplace.
I sing from the well we all drink from.
And along the paths we walk in dreams,
elephants, me and my boys.

Within minutes a young male appears
He is curious in his greeting,
pushing the scragginess aside,
wanting to see who is in the car
who is gifted to life, who dreams into
these cobalt blue sky places.

These are my sons. I say.
Birthed in soil and blood,
belonging poems of being

I speak their names.
Those sounds travel into the heat
and settle on the skin of the young bull.
He holds the moment, head lifted.

In a dream, weeks later, he tells me his name.
It is not a word I could write or say
It is made of sound petals that curl reddish
along paths between countries I have never been.
It is a life-giving name,
that means, when translated,
"always leave a pathway home".

My boys

I lie in my bed,
watching movies in my mind.
I see two anoraked and booted boys,
walking on a sand track to the stables.

Carrots for the horses,
fishing in the dam,
running through blue gums on yellow days,
reading in bed,
kites on the beach,
jumping on the trampoline.

The blooming of firsts - steps, words, reading,
canoes, skating, swims.

Love, sparkling life, on lakes and leaves
in shimmers of sunlight.

Both running to me, to be hugged
and scooped up, one on each hip,
like a harvest of good, blessed years.

My deepest gratitude is that you both
chose me to be your Mom.
It has been the poem of my life.

Mother's Day

I waken, tearful.
It's been too much,
this mother thing.
We'd no good history -
all of us broken
by men, by war, by work.
There was no grand, great, smiling,
happy someone somewhere,
carrying our DNA with delight.
Work and toil - our coat of arms.
We had odd days of dressing up,
celebrations, and then again
the bleak demands on us,
the women in grey photos,
my family, that travelled south,
hoping for more, but getting less.
This mother's day
my house is silent.

My dog sleeps next to me.
An ex-employee calls
to say thank you,
and the hot water, washing over
my kitchen sink hands,
promises me
we all did good,
despite the lack of praise.

Those women, my women,
loved and prayed and held children,
now grown up and ceded to life.
I lift my glass of juice
to all that I survived, with each one,
in the name of Mother.

May our anthem now be
clicks and birdsong,
sung with victory fists
in a landscape we hope to never leave
called mamma's motherland.

Now that you are 21

I am so proud of the peace
you carry. How you avoid
scratchiness in fabric and people.
You showed us that
the prizes aren't worth it
if they steal all your days.

Time's better spent
(except spending is not your word)
when it's loved for what it brings of itself,
when it's allowed to flower, to fruit, or not.

You showed us that leaves love, plants dream,
fish swim and the toast gets cold –
all in the now of things.

You keep your options open,
respecting the life each possibility holds.

I adore the flow of you, the sweetness
in your bright-brain-smart-heart humour.

Even as a small boy, you always connected,
seeing people, in the big country of their lives.

I wish you more and more
of what you carry in your heart.

I wish you great vistas of self-love
and the knowing of how much
you make the world better
in every one of your nows.

The Love of You

Today I remembered how, as a boy,
you would tell me your
favourite words.
Tractor. Lightyear. Samson.
Now that you live so far away, I am lost,
Tilted to your time zone
and your weather,
I miss your joy-gripping smile.
Your words now
Sydney, next-year, Julia.

4.

In the branches

The softness of death

I met death.
He has a soft side –
just like my dad in the veld.
Long socks, walking quietly,
looking, looking,
expecting a snake
to cross his path.
Death is here, now,
with clear intent
and kindness like water.
At my dad's bedside,
death's generosity has dark brown eyes
and a mean streak

The cupboard

When people say they came out
of the closet, I had a different
story to tell.

I hid in a cupboard,
behind long coats and dresses.
Because you took your big gun out
and shouted at my mom,
drunk and furious at her,
as if she was to blame
for the birthmark on your face.
Because you shot
the pretty blue guinea fowl
and ate it.
Because you stood unyielding,
always convinced you had the facts.
Because you showed laughing teeth,
calling us all cretins,
because you smelt like
spices and clean shirts,
and confusingly held my hand
when I was in trouble.

I stayed hidden in that
cupboard for a very long time
and never cared much for facts.

Initiation

I watched you, Granny,
strap your big wartime suspenders,
and your half-corset, as you dressed,
in a cloud of Johnson's talcum powder,
that went everywhere with you.
I stared at your long, bony legs
and big feet (now mine),
your hands, full-sized, from
too much cleaning, washing,
ironing, surviving.

A child in a British concentration camp,
you lost siblings, an aunt, and
your respect for the Queen.
Isn't she a mother? you would say.

You married a Jew called Joe,
and learnt to make chopped herring.
You survived the war, the depression,
his depression,
dragging my dad to the NG Kerk,
determined each day to be a decent,
god fearing, patriotic, good woman.

All of six years old, I asked,
Why do you wear those big panties?
To hide my stomach.

Why do you shake that powder?
To hide my woman smells.
What woman smells?
We all do that, you said,
we hide. One day you'll see.

Who are we hiding from, Granny?
Thinking it was hide and seek.
She burned her eyes into me:
Who do you think?
Wild animals? I ventured ... monsters?

Yes, wild animals and monsters, she said,
I call them men.

My recipe book

I looked into your eyes
to find my name,
my chants,
my recipe book,
 and saw only the windswept street
a grey day, and you
a little girl, looking
for your mom.

Crow

A crow flew above me
as I lay in the winter sun
alone at the women's baths.

I thought it was telling me
that my mother
had passed, as it winged and
dipped in, towards me.
I imagined that her crumbling spine
had finally betrayed her,
leaving me in seawater,
a sacred womb place of women
that she would never know.

Later, I flew across the ocean
to see her.
I knew the crow meant
change was coming.
On that grey airline seat,
I vowed always to watch
for signs of her aliveness
and not for her death.

In her room, hours later
I was still her child
even as I mothered her.
She was alive even as she,
the mom I knew,
had passed.

5.
Corporate moments

CEO moment

Shouting wildly,
you spat on me
We both watched your spit flying
in slow-motion
onto my jacket.

The sunlight glistened through its trajectory
in screaming slow motion
as I stood at your desk.

It flew over the licorice all sorts
and the board pack
and the resolution about your bonus.
It flew over your Swiss pen.
And tickets to Europe.

Those people, sort them out
today, you bellowed.

Sort hundreds of years of spit.
Ignore the spitters,
reign in the spat upon.

My privilege
was to be spat on
up close.

The rest
only got it
cascaded down like strategy.

Two real-life movies

You said you didn't hire women.
Your hands shot up – "They cry,
what do I do when they cry?"
You smiled.
Lord of the dirty world of sawn timber.

You held the words
like medals you won boxing.
Like a yellow card you were proud of.
They cry ... you muttered through your teeth.
Can't you see we are all men?

"What if I make YOU cry?"
I asked, in a loud, penis-less voice.
Your eyebrows danced.
"Haha ... you've got the job!"
And with that, I was hired.

You didn't know
that I grew up in cowboy movies,
shootouts in the street,
Tombstone and Deliverance.
I always had my posse.

I told you I'd dreamed you'd promised God
you'd be a Pastor.
You called me a witch.
You called yourself
a leadership legacy.
The rest of us called
it four-letter words,
like your name.

Your rage and promises to
cut lights, demolish lives built on hard shifts,
cold timber lives, was legendary.
You didn't know
that many people cursed you and even prayed you dead.
So it was Tombstone.

Did you finally get that job with God?
In that Covid nightmare,
did you ask forgiveness?
Was it Deliverance?

Job description: Lion tamer

My dad needed taming –
rogue, scarred, flea-bitten lion that he was.
I found a way to hush him
in a fearless mix of attack and praise.
So I got the job – Lion Tamer.
I developed techniques,
experimented with lion-whispering.

My next lion was my boss.
Like a rescue dog, almost rabid,
he suffered from mange of the heart.
I refined my strategy,
a little more gazelle, no rhino,
the same feigned fearlessness.

My heart beat loudly,
my body shouted run!
I faced, leaned in
teeth down, eyes on.
I shushed my heart, dead still.
Lions smell fear, shame and
most of all self-doubt.
I sprayed my version of
Jean Paul Gaultier behind my ears.

Trust me, with lions, you've got three choices,
three basic taming methods:
slash, dead-head or praise.
Each strategy is dangerous.

Slash is a head-on attack –
a show-down you need training for, expert skills to win.
Don't try this at home unless you tried it at home
your whole life.
Dead-head is to drop limp, dead voice,

no sign of life – a boring kill.
Praise is the easiest. Beware, it keeps them sniffing
for more and traps you like a prisoner.

My advice to all applicants for the Lion tamer position:
go with your gut and run.
It's a dying profession and the only career path,
a promotion to being a Lion.

C-Suite

She sat next to me on the flight
and held her jaw tight,
her busyness
and the menace of her deadlines
too big to be contained
by a simple seatbelt.
She reeked of having no time.

That give-away smell that cuts words,
shrinks stares into blinks,
shuts stories up
in bullet points.

I knew her little secret,
she didn't have time to pee or poo.
It's time we call it the P-Suite.

In spite of the NDA.

I had an English boss,
a bright, white-faced art collector,
with a wine farm and an indoor pool. In London.
He strolled through vineyards, while brokers begged
to speak to him, currencies fell,
and hedge funds were clipped like hydrangea bushes.
He went yachting with the royals.
He told me not to speak
to the servants.
It confuses them, he said.

I worked for a farmer,
who stuffed his well-fed toes
and fat racism into leather,
corporate shoes he'd bought in New York.

Stop talking if I look at you, he said,
watch my eyes for clues,
only tell the Board what we agree.
I know how to treat labour,
switch off their lights and water,
if they don't come around.
They shouldn't argue with us
in winter.

Real people living real lives,
imagining they had power,
every day, telling me what to do.

Women in suits

I salute you
I lift up the prayers you say,
the promises you keep,
the inching change you conjure,
the raids you make on the man-saturated
work mind

I salute the self you take to work,
believing the day for its promise,
despite being ambushed
again, and again
by foreheads of stone.

You are the single soldier
emerging from the Trojan horse,
holding both flowers and a sword,
the one who arrived early.

I salute you,
flagless on the mountain,
still you speak brave
knowing that change
takes a hero called
tomorrow.

7.
Another Life

The dream suburb

My neighbourhood
is dreaming time - I am awake there.
In dreams, my eyes see out of my belly
instead of my head.
My cousin Chris visits me, we play cards and joke.

People I know don't see me walking by.
When I wake up, my mind starts bossing me
to be more of exactly who I am, asleep.
Then,
my dreamface smiles like a stone,
my awake face puts on lipstick.

Who is who?
In the same moment
they both say: "Wakey wakey"
in stereo and laugh.

I forget whether I'm awake or asleep
and do just what I have to do
on my list marked
"Tuesday. Urgent"

I pronounce my body alive.

You held me while I cried alone.
You danced with me in all kinds of shoes.
You feasted delicious love with me.
You let song ignite your sinew,
tender, indescribable intimacies
have been yours.

Bitter coffee and sweet cake,
waterfall delights between smiling pine trees
have been yours.
Fabrics in colours and silk
and fresh air all over you,
as the sky covered you,
and the moon asked you
unanswerable questions.

You somehow knew how to birth my boys,
you knew when to run,
you heard the voice,
you felt the forest on fire.

At dawn you are still,
you breathe and open my heart,
sending out tiny dots of magic light.

Tell me anything. All my poems are listening.
I know what you want now.
You are the beloved in my arms.

Take me devoutly. Take me to death.
Take my prayers to the Goddess in the garden,
whisper my name, again and again,
in your limbs, your skin –
I'm listening at last.

Carlotti

You make tea for me,
bring me lunch,
and I work and work,
like a monk copying the Bible,
as if my job is
holy.
But it's love that
is holy.
You are the monk,
searching for truth
in our garden,
holding beauty like a
Siamese cat,
believing in the shape,
the colour and glory
of all that we breathe,
making warm-blooded
kindness and car music
holy.
While I am exhorting a
keyboard for money.
Absolution tastes like
fried egg on bread,
your gifts of man gentle
tenderness,
my blessings.

ICU

Don't go anywhere today.
Don't leave us, wailing
at your hospital bed.
Your DNA holds a poem
with your name on it,
a poem that can create
universes,
a song that is not finished
its singing.
It lights long pathways,
let its power rise.
It is holier than mosques, synagogues
and cathedrals, and hums a sound,
a quiet holy sound,
like a didgeridoo, in the very place
that you create from.
You hold that now.
I too am humming that tune
for you.
Hear it, sing it with me.
Please, it's not time for you
to say goodbye.
Rise, rise, rise.

Tanya

It's no surprise
that you come from Springs –
you understand
water may flow quickly,
or take many seasons.

"Both are good signs,"
you say, sitting on a stone wall
facing the sea,
hungry for laughter,
your belly filled with poems.

Springs watch how much
we have dared,
how we hold our warm bodies,
how we believe
in our breathing bones.

May your springs whisper
to your hips,
may they start dancing,
long before
the summer comes.

Nancy Reagan

Despite your perfect hair,
and embossed Whitehouse crockery,
you became my friend the instant I heard
your Godmother was a silent movie star.

I felt your ache for noise
and hugs, and plates
clattering during dinner.
Instead, you got thudsoft
footsteps on the carpet,
doors clicking, latches closing,
and furniture moving
in the upstairs room.
Your father moved out
before your first birthday

Your mother left,
preferring her acting career.
And dropped you,
a little bundle in New York,
with your aunt and
creepy uncle.
Your said your wordless
longing for your ma
grew bigger even than you.

Then I understood
your "Just say no."
This is the story of
a lonely girl.
You wanted her to
"Just say no",
to everything but you.

When healing comes

I smelt jasmine.
As close as the nose of a perfume bottle,
while you spoke, it flowered
from your story, and I, the hypnotist,
barely breathed
in case the smell took flight.

Time and space both opened,
to show the little girl you were
at the pool,
in a green costume with your mom.

The smell travelled 30 years
to kiss your forehead once again.
You said it was in bloom that day,
along with all the love you had forgotten.
A fragrant reminder of her gentleness,
remembered in an instant.

The trees and me

It dawned on me silently,
as I grew into being
a woman
that much of myself was
not me. It was for them.

I grew up learning
men were the lion and the rifle.
Men were guns and meat on the fire
Women were the salad.

I upheld this in conversations,
in years of micro-fawning
agreeing they were the ones
that deserved micro-more.
Micro-blinks of approval,
me colluding with my own
dissolving.

Until now.
I am the sea, and the sky.
the trees,
and I am me.

Asymmetry

Let's have a great love
- one that turns the suburbs
into Eden,
and the past
into nothing but
a preface for itself.
One that calls down
God and all his angels
into communion with life.

What about you?
What is it that you want
from coffee with
a stranger called me?

The dream

It is night and the dogs bark.
All is shadowy within, only the glimmer
of candles provides some flickering light.
I am in a cave of sandstone walls.
A candle lights your cheekbone momentarily,
just down the passage, as you turn away.
Did you call me, Shaykh?
I walk towards you
but you have left.
The cave has chamber after chamber.
The light is almost gone.
All I can follow is your fragrance.
I hear your cloak flutter
around a corner ahead
and your sandalwood smell grows stronger.
I cannot see nor discern the distance we cover
as you walk on the very edge of the air ahead of me.
I feel the chalky walls and come into a round room.
It is light and warm, furnished and carpeted.
Soft chanting comes from even deeper in the cave.
On the low table - figs, coffee.
I have never been here, but I am home.
I know I am to sleep
and awaken to be born,
to return from here
to my beginning.

Now the sunrise is calling me.
There is a note on the table
in Arabic - on textured paper.
I read it slowly, it's from
the Shaykh.
"Listen to me. Don't listen to anyone else"
I breathe out.
I turn the soft paper over.

On the other side, more Arabic,
dancing on the page.
"Don't listen to me."

My man Loneliness

Let me tell you about my man
Loneliness.
He has a seductive scent,
he plucks a tune on his guitar,
hums softly, dances slowly
takes off all his clothes.
He whispers ...
and I cha cha cha,
singing French-Spanish
love-my-life songs.

In the morning light
I find I am alone.
I discover my hands
were filled with
scarecrow sticks,
my taffeta dress
was dry leaves,
the silk of his suit
was the sheen of veld grass.
As the sun sweats,
just one buzzard in the sky
is cutting north.
I am utterly alone.
The silence is a high sky,
with clouds floating
dead and beyond.
No sound and nobody.

Later I find a note
next to my bed. It's from my man,
my man Loneliness.

"Dear Woman - in the moonlight,
don't fight me. I know you.

I'm in the lines of all your poems,
I'm the taste of your mouth
after kissing,
and the smell
of your freshly made bed.
I'm in all the lists you ever made,
and in the tickets for the show.
I'm the coins
in the drawer of your desk,
I'm the edge that makes
that horizon,
the colour of the storm.

I'm the one that knows you best.
Embrace me again
like a lover,
I'll sing you wild old songs.
Embrace me.
We dance so well together.
Your body calls, your heart begs.
I know all
the places you call home.

So I cha cha cha,
singing, slow dancing
love-my-life songs.

8.
I'm ready to travel

To us

This blood flows in us,
hidden in our veins,
it knows what we do not.
Like Saxons, like trampled roses,
looking north, south,
to the pole star, to the sun,
it now flows uncharted,
to places undreamed and unspoken.

Some of us from Dresden,
some from Spain, some spoke Yiddish,
sang German, choked mud,
hiding on battlefields, in veldt,
cried out, in prison in Ceylon.
Anglo and Boer.

Some of us drank fermented beer.
Believing boer legends true on far horizons.
Some baked soetkoekies,
learnt sonnets, washed and ironed,
reached beyond poverty and drink,
to the spark of a deeper life

The rousing chorus across our blood
is the anthem, a call to arms, a cry
for an expansive, exhaled, gentle life.

Us all, all shamans, travelling through time
in spirit and elephant-knowledge.
May our bloodline be the zebra that leads you
to water, and may all that is good
resurrect in your cells to bless you
with what we, and our alive ancestors,
still call freedom.

Instant life

The morning proclaims a stark and freezing freedom.
The cold is waiting outside like a lover
wanting to strip me bare.

I am afraid I may be too unlustful
for its all-seeing eyes, its strong, groping fingers,
I'm too cosy in my coat.

And yet I want the exile.
My desire demands that I ditch my subscriptions,
my comfort, and run.

Take me to the freezing edge of me –
I know there is a map I haven't seen,
uncharted in its longing, I dart outside quickly,
pulling off my coat, my top, my naked breasts greet the street,
the ice grabs me full-fingered, the day stands still.

A car hoots. The sun beats.
Another life
has happened in an instant.

Wollumbin Retreat

The first night

It's 3 am
I dream that I'm walking
to the water far beyond the forest
It's blue dark and warm
I wait there silently as the dingo shadows emerge
Moving across the land towards me
Calling me to follow, follow the river, follow the dreamline
We are all moving through the night.

I don't know where to step
I am clouded
My heart aches from
Unpunished good deeds
Demanding reparation
And my dream wakes me.

Here, words that usually hang
Like mass produced Chinese flip flops
In the air of everydayness
Become shining lanterns
Of belonging.

Dingo take me deeper into the formless
Silence where shapes are stilled by trees
Your dream maps glisten in plain sight
I am ready to travel now
Birds echo frog sounds on quartz spiral pathways
And my ears perch on my head
Ready for flight.

Last day

I look in the mirror
after my shower and dab my face.
It's the face of a person called poet.

I did not arrive here with that blessing
lodged between my limbs,
like hope shoved into a Jerusalem wall.

> I came here with a gap
> between those stones.
> Filled for me now, anew.

Last poem

I long to rebel against my voice.
Trapped in one corral of words,
I knock against
the fence and poles.

My two-eyed noticing blinds me,
while the extraordinariness
of what I know nothing about
sweeps and falls in ways
I cannot imagine.

I will crack my knowing like an egg
and run my fingers through the yolk,
feeling for the braille of a life unlived.
I will place cucumbers on my nipples
and a sports bra over my eyes.
I will write tiny poems on rose petals
and drink them in tea.
I will inject sunrise like Botox
into my cheekbones,
and stir away the green,
stagnant scum that blocks
fresh air from my overweight tongue

until I can speak triumph
in the blue-breasted language
of a kingfisher
and vow silence
to the morning dew.

Afterword

Wind Spirit

When I die,
let it be into death's open embrace,
without shame for the full length of me,
without dread for the faces that wait.
Ready for my heart to be weighed,
pulled like a ballet muscle into bliss.
I will be received into that chamber
of the afterlife, with words.

Words in this life have asked much of me,
required me to walk into spider webs
that scared me, letting the flesh-ugly spider
crawl onto my bare neck.
In death, they will require thresholds and gates,
where every password is forgotten,
where every watchword glows.
I saw swans floating on a canal
in the moonlight and I knew
they swam the beauty of the silent, after-life words.

Nowadays, my own words come slowly,
peeping out of their meaning–shells.
I believe their power to create.
Each word an archaeology of being,
an embryo touching the eyelashes of the heart.
The one Heart.

Come in, come in, you, to the word sound.
Follow a djembe bird call, a beetle trail,
the buzz of the lawnmower.
Creep into the embroidery of woven grass,
just to hear and to speak, to birth a word,
birth it, before the swans come.

Find the words your own mouth sings,
the grammar of your own back yard.
Find the words of your fingerprint,
and let them take you far.
We have a sound line, a word line, a lifeline.
It is a path to the arches of truth.
You've been there,
I saw you at the fountain.

www.ingramcontent.com/pod-product-compliance
Lightning Source LLC
Chambersburg PA
CBHW071240090426
42736CB00014B/3155